Daniel A. Warner, PhD

Associate Professor of OT & Archeology

New Orleans Baptist Theological Seminary

What a wonderful story of life changing proportions One is always amazed of how God uses people, the story has repeated itself for thousand of years. A person takes Christ as their savior through the words of another, then God uses them to share in places one would never think of being able to go. The author's accounts demonstrate clearly God's power and unique opportunities. It was a joy to read.

++++++++++

Reverend Ken Taylor

Campus Bible Fellowship Staff

The book "When you Hear the Cry of the Lost" is an inspiring account of how God developed a heart full of compassion for the lost souls of this world in the heart of a faithful servant, shared through personal life stories and poems.

++++++++++

Reverend Gary Sammons,
Missionary with Baptist Mid-Missions

"When You Hear the Cry of the Lost" comes straight from the heart of a woman consumed with the passion not only to win the lost to Christ all over the world, but also to stir others to have that burden. The book contains Maria's evangelistic experiences all over the world. They are woven together to show how the Great Commissioner can use anyone who loves Him and listens to His heart-beat for the lost. The author's poetry in the concluding section will inspire the reader to sense the value, need and urgency of evangelism.

Dr. Bob Jakoby

Chaplain, Miami Baptist Hospital

Corporate Director of Pastoral Care

Baptist Health Systems of So. Florida

Hearing the "Cry of the Lost" is God's call to every believer in Christ! Maria has heard His call and is following Him wherever He leads at whatever the cost. She inspires and challenges the reader through her faith and dependence on the Holy Spirit'.

The author's love and passion for Christ and lost souls is contagious. The power of Christ is evident in her boldness to share Christ with others and it will encourage the reader to do the same!

++++++++++

Becky Jakoby

Maria's passion for the lost is undeniable as she expressed herself so beautifully in this book. It is an inspiration to us all who as believers should have the same passion to carry the message to the world. Throughout her writing it is clear that the Holy Spirit is the one who enables her. The same is true for all of us if we are willing and available to be used.

++++++++++

Reverend Rick Lee

Former Missionary to Brazil

Pastor Homestead Mennonite Church

One saint's journeys as she shares the love of Jesus with a world of people desperate to be loved. Maybe you will be moved to love and to share as well.

++++++++++

Rev. Ronald Brummitt,

President Miami Rescue Mission / Broward Outreach Centers

"When You Hear The Cry Of The Lost" will reignite your passion for witnessing and rekindle your prayers for a world that needs Jesus. I have known Maria for over twenty years and am amazed of how God took her around the world to proclaim the Gospel to so many. Her story demonstrates how God can work through His children if we are only open and obedient to Him. May God stir the hearts of all who read to respond to the cry of the lost.

++++++++++

It is with real joy that I endorse this book written by my good friend. Her passion for lost souls is contagious and it is obvious that God has given her the gift of evangelism. Her memory of the various encounter are precise . God has given her a bold spirit in witnessing and a keen understanding of scriptural truths. Reading this book will bless and encourage your heart.

In His Royal Service,

Dr. David R. Crandall

International Director

Answers WorldWide

When You Hear The Cry Of The Lost

Cultivating a passion for souls

by

Gladys “Maria” Sotomayor Booth

Copyright © 2011 by Gladys "Maria" Sotomayor Booth

When You Hear The Cry Of The Lost
Cultivating a passion for souls
by Gladys "Maria" Sotomayor Booth

Printed in the United States of America

ISBN 9781619960183

All rights reserved solely by the author. The author guarantees all contents are original and do not infringe upon the legal rights of any other person or work. No part of this book may be reproduced in any form without the permission of the author. The views expressed in this book are not necessarily those of the publisher.

Unless otherwise indicated, Bible quotations are taken from the New King James Version of the Bible.

www.xulonpress.com

CONTENTS

ACKNOWLEDGMENT

I remember the first time I met this humble servant of the Lord. We had recently moved to Kendall and were looking for a church for our family to attend. One day my son in law came home and very enthusiastically told us he believed he had found a church for us not too far from our house. He said it was still under construction but that he had stopped by and the Pastor had invited him to come back with the family to the service that same night. We Accepted the invitation to attend the service and that same night met Pastor Arnold Warner, who immediately became our friend and mentor.

This godly man and his wife Jean built the sanctuary, but most importantly they built a church. Pastor's love and unselfish dedication to serve others was an example to all. He was the one who taught me that: "It's not about me." Maybe he never even made the statement, but his life modeled it. It was never about him, it was always about others. The way he lived left an indelible mark in me and inspired me to go and tell others about Jesus and His love without fear or hesitation. It also stirred the right thoughts and reflections that eventually resulted in this book.

+++

To David Crandall I owe everything I know about missions. Therefore, I'm entitled to say that Dr. Crandall has been the wind beneath my missionary wings. Without him I wouldn't have had anything to write about in this book. He was there for me from the beginning of the journey and hopefully will also be there when it ends. Thank you brother David.

+++

Special thanks to Carlos Licona, my nephew and brother in Christ, who stood beside me from the time this book was a mere thought. His prayers and faithful support were always encouraging. He also painstakingly donated his time and computer expertise to help make this book a reality.

+++

Finally my deepest gratitude goes to Janell Gover, a friend for all seasons. Although not blood related in human terms, we are spiritually blood related because we are covered by the same blessed blood of Jesus. Thank you sister for your prayers and continuous support. Just listening to you inspired me to keep laboring and to remain joyful and victorious in our Lord Jesus Christ.

Dedication

To my children

Donald, Janine and Arnie

My grandchildren,

Donnie, Kenny and Meghan

"Let all that you do be done in love."

1Corinthians 16:14

and

To my many relatives and friends who

stayed behind and prayed each time I left to

tell others about Jesus and His love

"To open their eyes and to turn them from darkness to light, and from the power of Satan unto God, that they may receive forgiveness of sins, and inheritance among them which are sanctified by faith that is in me"

Acts 26:18

Preface

The story begins the day I heard for the first time about missions in a personal way. My Church had invited Dr. David Crandall, the International Director of Gospel Literature Services to speak to us. He told us about the millions of lost souls across the globe searching in vain without hope and how Christians moved by the Holy Spirit were responding to the call to share with them the Good News of Jesus Christ and His love.

His passion and enthusiasm was undoubtedly due to the sincerity of his commitment to obey the Great Commission. I know that every one in our Church was moved by his words. I for one immediately realized that my life was being changed. I felt a sudden wave of love and compassion rising in my heart and the urgent desire to go and tell others about Jesus. As soon as the service was over I met with our guest speaker and his wife and volunteered to join them in their next mission trip.

This was the year 2000 and the Summer Olympics were in Sidney, Australia. This was my first missionary trip and the timing was perfect because an event like this provided the opportunity to reach out to people from all over the world, that would be there either participating in the Olympic Games or sports fans attending the different athletic events.

Since then, my love for Jesus really began to bloom and as a result He has allowed me to go on other missions, among them two more Olympic missions to Athens, Greece and Vancouver, Canada. These Olympic missions give us the unique advantage to contact people from all over the world in a pleasant and festive environment. What a great opportunity to approach the subject of worldly pleasures and temporal satisfaction versus heavenly treasures and eternal fulfillment.

As a servant of the Lord my greatest desire is to be used by Him. Every mission trip has been an exercise in faith and endurance. I have seen the hand of God in every step taken and in every challenge that we faced. The essence of our purpose is the reality of hell. If you do not repent of your sins and accept Jesus as your Savior, you go to hell when you die. If you repent and give your life to Jesus, when you die you go to be with Him forever.

This is a simple concept and the principal motivator to go to the unbelievers in every corner of the earth. If we love others we don't want them to burn in hell for eternity. So we must go to them no matter where they are and tell them about Jesus and His love. With prayer and supplication we must go to the Lord and ask the Holy Spirit to indwell us and lead us by faith to the lost souls who are waiting for salvation in our own backyard or in another far away land.

We have arrived at a time in history where we must make our words heard before we depart. Our stay in this world is beginning to be shortened and the days left must be urgently spent by obeying God's Command to share the Gospel. Accepting the hardships and removing the obstacles we are called to march forward proclaiming

His Word wherever we go. Remember silence is never heard.

Although still strangers in this world, still rejected and persecuted, now is not the time to stop. By tolerating corrupted doctrines and mundane philosophies and reconciling these heresies to our Christian beliefs, in order to be liked and accepted, we have done nothing but compromise our Christian principles and cause corruption and dissention among the Saints. We are Christian soldiers ready to wear the Armor of God and proceed to conquer the lost world in the name of Jesus Christ, our Lord and our Savior.

Whether we go abroad or stay home we can all be part of the same team and under the same divine plan of conquering the world for Jesus Christ. Like the great missionary to India, William Carey once said to his friends and supporters "I will go down if you'll hold the ropes." To which I add, I'll fervently pray for those holding the rope. I don't think I need to explain why.

And like the title of this book I will continue to proclaim to those of you who are called to go, to listen carefully and you will hear the Cry of the Lost.

Sometimes is so soft you have to listen hard

Sometimes is like a child crying and it breaks your heart

Sometimes is just a murmur from really, really far

Sometimes sounds like a shout coming from the wild

But no matter how it really sounds

It is always the desperate cry

Of a lost soul looking for a way out

Reaching out to God, breaking down the walls

SECTION ONE

+++++

Answering His Call

The more you love the Lord, the more you will love the lost! If you love the Lord and you love others as He commands us to do, then you will love the lost.

More than a religion, Christianity is a relationship of the heart. God has replaced our heart of stone with a new heart. A heart that feels the needs of the lost humanity around us is exactly what the Lord desires for all His children.

If you feel the need of those around you who live without God, then you know that you can also hear their cry for help, "The Cry of the Lost." I venture to say that when we become deaf to the groans of a dammed soul, we commit a sin. This happens when we become insensitive to the need of others. . We become callous simply because we lack love.

The moment we cease to focus in ourselves we are transformed from a selfish existence to a glorious life with Christ. "It is in Christ that we find out who we are and what we are living for. Long before we first heard of Christ.....He had His eye on us, had designs on us for glorious living, part of the overall purpose He is working out in everything and everyone." Ephesians 1:11

The love for the lost is really a supernatural love; because only through Christ can we love the unlovable and show compassion to the sinner. This is why we do everything for His glory so they may see Christ in us.

We were made by God and for God....and until we understand that, life will never make sense. I know because this is what happened to me when I finally realized that I live only to serve Him. My life changed and this is how.

HE MADE ME MORE COMPASSIONATE

I began to see the hurt and the pain all around me, people were not just simply people. They became souls bound to hell unless they repented and accepted Jesus as Savior. Therefore, wherever He opened doors, I went and evangelized. To places like Israel and Jordan and most of Europe, including various former soviet republics and also closer to home, like Guatemala and the Dominican Republic. He took me to three Olympic Games in Australia, Greece and Canada; where people from many different countries accepted the Lord.

MY RELATIONSHP WITH GOD GREW CLOSER

My life became a journey with an assignment to be fulfilled. The journey became pleasant because I knew He was the source of my inspiration and my daily sustenance. My prayer routine became a conversation between friends and we remain in closed contact throughout the day.

THE STRESS OF LIFE ENDED

For the first time I really understood the words of Philippians 4:-7 "......and the peace of God that surpasses all understanding" really filled my heart and mind. I became more relaxed and confident once I learned to trust Him no matter what the circumstances are.

WORDS BECAME WORKS

Volunteering at the Veterans Hospital and at public schools became so enjoyable that I hated to leave and go home. Before, I was reluctant to get involved in politics, but now I began to pay more attention and realized that this was also an important part of my life. As a Christian, it is also my duty to participate in the democratic process of electing our leaders according to our principles and beliefs. Thus, I became more interested in the affairs of government and unafraid to speak up. Now I write letters to government officials, newspaper editors and party representatives. I have even written to two U.S. Presidents and the Pope. Only the Lord knows if my efforts have had an effect on the outcome of any of the issues I defend or protest, but the fact that I'm doing my duty is good enough for me. I only trust and obey, the rest is in His hands.

BECOMING BOLD AND COURAGEOUS

Since I'm on a mission from God and God is my Commander, I have no fear. I have witnessed to people in airports, airplanes, market places, department stores, grocery stores, hospitals, theaters and in my own neighborhood. The last being the most difficult. When we finally conclude that we need to focus on Christ and not in ourselves, our lives will be fulfilled and it is then that we are able to stop searching for a meaningful life. Once I learned and accepted this fact, I have lived with peace and contentment. Sharing my joy with everyone around me gives me great satisfaction. Life continues to bring tribulations, but without the doubts and uncertainties that I experienced before, I have peace. I know my God is in control!

DIVINE APPOINTMENT IN SIDNEY

We had been invited by the Australian Baptists to help them organize an event to distribute gospel literature and witness to Sydney's Olympic guests. We had prepared by printing millions of copies of Christian tracts in fifteen different languages, and organizing an army of sixty-five Christian volunteers, the youngest one being only 13-years old.

Australia has shown a great resistance to the gospel and is therefore, spiritually needy. We were also aware of the fact that because of the Olympic Games, there were going to be international visitors from about 200 different countries, including many pagan countries. What a great opportunity to deliver the Good News to a godless world.

Our expectations were really high and with God's blessings we knew we could not be disappointed. This was the attitude of the American team when we joined our Australian brothers and sisters at the local Baptist Church serving as our headquarters.

After we prayed together and briefly introduced both teams, we were on our own. By the end of the meeting, it was only one team. We had combined our spiritual and material resources into one big but well organized crowd of enthusiastic Christians. After the initial briefing we divided into teams, met our house guests, picked up our load of Bibles and other Christian literature, we were ready to meet any challenge, any time, anywhere.

My host family was a deeply committed Christian couple with two small children and one on the way. Another lady from my team and I were staying with them for the two weeks we were in Sidney. From the very beginning we were made to feel at home, the entire family, including the two little ones, was extremely happy to have us staying with them.

Because our new home was in a different town, not too far from our mission headquarters, at the end of the day, we had to walk to the train station and take a train to the next town where our host would promptly pick us up. Not matter how late it was, he would be there, smiling and inviting us to have tea with him and his wife. Although we had already had dinner at the Church, we still enjoyed meeting with them and eating some great Australian home-made dessert.

Every morning we did the same thing in reverse and when we arrived at our destination, someone would be waiting for us to give us a ride to the church. Our day began with hearty breakfast and great morning service and after taking care of the logistics for the day we embarked in our mission. A big bus would take us to downtown Sidney and drop us off, we would then walk to the different venues we had been assigned.

Every day was a spiritual adventure. We sang at malls, walked the crowded streets, started conversations with players from different countries, passed literature to the sports fans and visitors and prayed with them. In other words, we claimed for Jesus the most beautiful harbor in the world, Sydney Harbor and everything in it. As a result, many were led to the Lord right there and were saved, while others took the tracts and Bibles home with them. We believe that when we are all in heaven we'll find out how many of these souls converted later.

One time I sat down on a bench at a local park in Sidney to rest a while, when I noticed an oriental looking girl sitting next to me. I smiled at her and she gently smiled back and resumed her reading. For some reason I thought this beautiful girl seemed lonely, so I quietly began to pray for her.

When I turned around she had stop reading and was looking at me and this time she said hello and pretty soon we were talking to each other. She told me her name was Naka and that she was from Japan. She said she had come to Australia to study English, but that she had not made any friends and missed her family very much.

Naka was soft spoken and shy, but seemed interested in continuing the conversation, so I began to tell her about my best friend Jesus and how He had changed my life completely. I shared with her how a group of Christians like me had come to Sydney to tell others about Christ and that were like a big family because we had the same Father.

From this moment on Naka's demeanor changed completely. She became alive and began to ask questions, she wanted to hear more about Jesus. She said she had known some Christians in Japan, but had never paid much attention to what they had to say. But now it was different, I knew I had all her interest and attention, so I began to tell her about Jesus and His love for all of us.

I read the sinner's prayer from my tract and Naka repeated after me. Then she spoke a few sentences in Japanese and looked up at me smiling and said "new Naka". We hugged each other and with tears in our eyes began to laugh. I got her full name and address and we promised to keep in touch. I told her that she was going to hear from a local pastor for spiritual guidance and growth. I also told her that she was going to meet other Christians that would become like her own family for they would be her brothers and sisters in Christ.

Later that evening, I got on my knees and thanked our Lord for Naka's conversion. Once again I realized that all that had occurred was predestined, that I had served as an instrument of God to bring salvation to another soul. It was a supernatural event, a divine appointment made in Heaven.

There were many more people saved during our Olympic journey, among them a coach from the Colombian soccer team. This gentleman accepted Jesus in front of several of his team players. Again, this was another divine appointment. When we met, he was on his way to have lunch with his team. So we can proudly say that he met the Lord on his way to eat and his life was forever changed.

We had so much happening in Sidney it would take more than a chapter to tell it all. Suffice to say that more than successful the mission was blessed with great success. It was a time in the lives of all of us who attended, not to be ever forgotten. It was like a legion of angels were right there with us, aiding us, guiding us, encouraging us and rejoicing with us every time a lost soul was saved and Satan was defeated.

I cannot tell you the results of any of the Olympic Games, nor the names of any of the famous players who won Olympic medals, but I can tell you that the group of humble Christian missionaries who came back home were all winners. We will pick up our gold medals and prizes later on in Heaven!

THE GOSPEL SHAKES ATHENS

The Athens Olympic ministry officially began when all 139 team members from across the U.S. and Canada began traveling towards Greece to take up where the Apostle Paul left off 2000years ago. Our mission was to spread the good news of salvation through faith in Christ Jesus alone to a lost world during the 2004 Summer Olympic Games.

When we arrived in Athens we had a long delay because all the Christian literature and "gospel bracelets" we had shipped ahead of us were confiscated by custom officials. They were emphatically claiming that these bracelets had a trade value and therefore we should pay a tariff. Again, the hand of God was with us when our representative got the clever idea to compare our bracelets to be similar to their "worry beads", to be solely used for praying. After emphasizing that they were to be given away and not for sale, the custom officials declared the items to be duty- free.

We figured it would have cost a considerable amount of money and further delay if this matter had not been resolved, so we promptly gathered together and thanked our Lord for intervening in our behalf. We continued celebrating our victory by singing and praising the Lord. We were definitely motivated to spread the Word of God all over this land, we felt invincible because we had the Holy Spirit in us.

While in Athens we stayed at an Evangelical Christian camp overlooking the Aegean Sea. The camp was about 100 miles from Athens and it took a couple of hours to get there. Every morning we were transported to the city of Athens by bus and brought back each evening after spending a glorious day.

Each day we divided up into 13 teams with 10 on a team. Each team had a team leader and was assigned a different area each day. Our daily schedule was the same each day. Up at 6:00 a.m. breakfast together at the camp, prayer and worship time. After that we promptly got ready and gathered our daily supplies of literature tracts, Bibles etc. We also carried our lunch and plenty of water. We had dinner somewhere downtown in the city with the rest of our team and afterwards headed back to our camp. The ride back was very pleasant because we were tired but exceedingly happy because our efforts had been rewarded.

We witnessed to many people. Some were Greeks and some were Olympic game officials or athletes from different countries and some were sports enthusiasts and spectators. Among the many that I witnessed to, eleven accepted Christ. They were three teen girls from Germany, two young men from Iraq, one lady from Ethiopia, one young couple from Albania and three ladies from Greece, one of them a clerk at the local bank where I had gone with brother Paul to exchange our dollars for euros.

I just have to take the time to tell this story because it literally changed the lives of two people. It is undisputable that their lives on earth were totally affected and of course, their eternal lives assured.

This particular day, our team had been assigned to the beach in Athens.

By the time we arrived at the beach, that very hot and windy day, I was already feeling tired and a little frustrated. We had been walking up and down the beach aimlessly searching for those we were supposed to lead to Jesus. Instead, all we had found were a lot of discarded Christian tracts, meaning that the people who had received them were trashing them. We even found a Bible next to a trash can. Although we had anticipated that the beach crowd was going to be a little rough, we still felt hurt and disappointed.

After a while our leader gathered our team together and we prayed for wisdom and strength, both physical and spiritual. Afterwards, we decided to move to another part of the beach. We soon discovered though, that this move was another mistake. Apparently this was a private sector with beach clubs and loud entertainment, therefore we moved again.

By now I was really physically tired and a little grumpy. I couldn't believe we were still here wasting time and supplies when we could have been back in the city where the crowds were a lot more approachable. I had my eyes closed while I prayed and complained, therefore I had not noticed that someone was attentively looking at me. It was a young man with black curly hair and a big smile on his face. I understand his being amused by the crazy lady wearing a button-down yellow shirt and kaki pants, a straw hat and carrying a big backpack, talking to herself while standing among the many scarcely-dressed bathers. Very funny!

Anyway, curly-hair kept smiling, so since I already had his attention, I decided to go and talk to him. Not knowing what language he spoke, I tried English first and he gestured no with his head, but was still smiling. I was not giving up yet, so I showed him a few of the different-language tracts that I was carrying in my back pack, pointing out to several, while he kept saying "no" with his head. Then he said something that sounded familiar to my Spanish-trained ears, it was Italian. Immediately I gave him a tract written in Italian.

Somehow we communicated in his broken Italian, my Spanish and his broken English. I learned that his name was Rani, and he had come to Athens with friends, that he spoke Arabic and some Italian and that his friend had come with him but had just left momentarily. He was very curious about me, so I told him I was a Christian who had come from America with some friends to tell people about Jesus and His love. I signaled "praying with my hands" and pointed to Jesus up in the sky and this way we managed to continue our very unusual conversation.

When his friend joined us, Rani and I were already friends. He immediately talked to him in a different language and pointing to me introduced us. To my great surprise, his friend spoke English fairly well, therefore our communication improved and I found out they were Muslims.Once again a miracle occurred when the Holy Spirit took over from then on and after a few minutes "with prayer and supplication and with thanksgiving, we brought our request to the Lord, and the peace of God that surpasses all understanding filled our hearts and minds in Christ Jesus" (Phil:6-7), and the two young Iraqi men, Rani and Sizar, former Muslims, asked Jesus to forgive their sins and come into their hearts.

Greater joy, I had never experienced! They were incredibly happy. Their entire demeanor had changed from humorous skeptics and doubters to blessed believers. We exchanged information, I gave each a Bible and pamphlets in Italian, English and Spanish. I also wrote their names, addresses, and phone numbers to keep in contact and continue ministering and aiding them in their spiritual growth. I know for sure that extensive follow-up have been done on these two men and they continue to respond and grow in faith and grace.

The following day, we had been scheduled to spend one day in Corinth. Corinth was especially interesting to all of us because it is here where the Apostle Paul preached to the Greeks about their "unknown God" and where he faced his accusers before the Roman Pro-Consul Gallio as described in Acts 18. So this beautiful day instead of dividing into teams, all of us traveled together to this history-filled city and ministered to the gentiles just as Paul had done so many years ago.

The ministry of the Olympic Games is incredible challenging and rewarding opportunity for every Christian who wants to reach the world for Christ. I, for one will always be grateful to the Lord for giving me the opportunity to go and bring the Word of God to people from all over the world. We saw about 79 people profess Christ as Savior and witnessed to hundreds more.

We must continue praying for the Greek believers, pastors and missionaries because normally they wouldn't be allowed to witness the way we did. The Greek Orthodox Church is the official church of the nation of Greece and is therefore protected by the authorities. Because of the Olympic Games they relaxed some of their laws to accommodate the other countries and their different cultures. Many Greek believers face daily persecution and we know that many of the new Christians would most likely find very hard to live a Christian life.

Twice during our mission, the police tried to stop us. The first time fortunately the incident was resolved when a high ranking government official intervened on our behalf, however the team was still expelled from Mars Hill, and was not able to witness there that day. The next day it was our team's turn to visit Mars Hill and witness. This time though, we had decided not to wear our uniforms to avoid being easily spotted. We were the largest group of Americans in the city and because of our yellow polo shirts, were known as the "Yellow Shirts".

The day before our departure we almost got in the middle of an anti-American demonstration in front of the Parliament Building in Athens, but we left promptly before anything happened. The next day when we passed through the troubled area, we saw the popular McDonald's Restaurant, where we had eaten many times before, partially burned and destroyed.

We left Athens, but we know for sure the Word of God stayed behind, changing lives and bringing hope and redemption to the lost. For a season we were ambassadors for Christ in Greece and when our mission ended the results of our labor were evident because the seeds that we planted were already beginning to sprout. Thus, we need more laborers to harvest the fields in Greece and everywhere in the land. "Then Jesus said to them, "The harvest truly is great, but the laborers are few, therefore pray the Lord of the harvest to send out laborers into His harvest". Luke 10:2

REACHING OUT TO EASTERN EUROPE

Despite resistance to the Gospel, the churches and believers in this part of Europe are committed to spread the Word of God. These are heroes of the faith that despite of limited resources and unbelievable obstacles continue to carry out the Great Commission.

The history of the Gospel in this region is stained with the blood shed by Christian martyrs, such as Jan Hus who was condemned for heresy and set on fire by the Catholic Church, here in Prague, almost 600 years ago.

We were here to visit the Czech Republic, Slovakia, Hungary and Austria. Our team of nineteen Americans, ranging in age from twenty-seven to eighty-one was divided into five teams traveling to four different countries to give spiritual support to national pastors and missionaries, encourage church planting in the region and join the local churches in their quest to reach lost souls.

Once we arrived at our destination, we divided into teams and received our assignments. There were three of us in our team and our first mission was to visit a Gypsy church in Zsambok, Hungary. From this point on my spiritual journey began. Meaning, that although I had been on several missionary trips before, nothing compared to the spiritually-charged encounter I experienced at this gypsy community.

These believers are double outcasts because they are not only rejected by their own countrymen who consider them the lowest class of society, but they are also shunned by other Gypsies because they are now Christians.

The small congregation met in Pastor Freddy's house because they have not been able to build their church yet, however, this did not curtail their determination and enthusiasm to gather and worship the Lord.

This particular day, we were already in the house, talking to Pastor Freddy and his family when the people started to arrive. They were in groups of several families, with children, older people, young adults, and teens all laughing, talking and smiling as they approached the house.

The little house came alive the moment the singing and praising started. Although I couldn't understand a word we all sang together... There were flutes, guitars, drums, tambourines and even a young man banging a kitchen pot. To our amazement, the loud noise of so many instruments sounded beautiful and harmonious. I could just see Jesus smiling at us! We could feel His holy presence surrounding all of us with His love. Although lit only by one light, Pastor Freddy's living room was shining, as if it were on fire.

After about forty-five minutes of pure rejoicing, they asked one of our missionaries to preach. Inspired by such a loving congregation, our preacher delivered a magnificent sermon. He emphasize that although they were being persecuted and mistreated, these young believers were chosen by Jesus Christ himself, and therefore were part of a divine plan to keep the faith and continue trusting God because they were already blessed and part of God's Kingdom.

After witnessing the blind faith and pure love of the Gypsy community, we continued our journey with more zeal and enthusiasm. The experience had given us a sense of urgency and increased our desire to continue our mission of ministering to the lost.

Once again we were reminded by our Lord, that although we thought we had come to be providers, we were instead receivers.

I lost count of the days for we were here and there and everywhere. All I remember is that the days were intense and every experience very rewarding. I also remember feeling immensely happy. We traveled as a group by train, by bus and by car, always praying and singing or just making joyful noises when we were very tired. We prayed together every morning and every evening met again to share the highlights of the day and thank God for all that happened.

We had sent to Europe several boxes of Christian literature in six different languages before we departed and they were there waiting for us when we arrived. So we had enough material to distribute among the churches we visited and also to pass out to people as we travel the continent.

It was one of these pamphlets that I gave to Esther, a shop clerk in Szentendre, a Hungarian village we were visiting. To my delight, Esther became very interested in reading the tract because it was written in her own language. She looked at me surprised and started asking me to tell her more about Jesus. Although she spoke little English, she seemed to understand clearly what I was saying and pretty soon we were involved in a vibrant conversation. At this point I knew I had to share the Good News with her. After explaining the plan of salvation I asked her if she wanted to accept Jesus as her Lord and Savior and she immediately said "Yes, yes, I do"

After all the excitement was over, she readily gave me her name and her e-mail address so one of the local missionaries could contact her later. I then started thanking my Lord Jesus for the salvation of another soul and was immediately filled with that peace that surpassed all understanding.

It is still hard for me to explain what occurs when a Christian leads a soul to the waiting arms of Jesus, because it is really beyond human comprehension. Let me just say that is a supernatural moment of triumph when even the angels in heaven rejoice.

The next day during our morning devotional we thanked our Lord for allowing us to come to the mission field and embrace new cultures and different people and for allowing us to travel from so far away to tell them that Jesus Christ loves them even more that we do.

The trip back home was uneventful. We were mostly quiet, reminiscing about the journey and all the wonderful things we had witness and all the souls that were saved because we had boldly proclaimed the Word of Jesus!

Once again we headed back home immersed in our unforgettable thoughts while experiencing immense joy and "the peace of God that surpasses all understanding".

THE HOLY LAND EXPERIENCE

For a Christian, visiting the Holy Land cannot be described any other way but as an experience, a life changing experience and this is why.

The moment we arrived at Israel Ben Gurion Airport in Tel Aviv we knew this journey was going to be different. Our group of thirty-three weary travelers came alive the moment we hit the ground, we could hardly believe we had finally arrived. After all we were going to be traveling for the next few days through the land where Jesus was born, where He lived, died and resurrected, and we could hardly hold back our emotions.

The first city we visited was Caesarea. We arrived by bus to a most beautiful historical site and visited the amphitheater and the Aqueduct. Caesarea is a city north of Tel Aviv, built by Herod to honor Caesar. It was here where Peter first presented the Gospel to the Gentiles when he preached to Cornelius (a Roman centurion) and his family.

We left for Mt. Carmel where Elijah confronted the prophets of Baal and God answered his prayers with fire from Heaven. From this mountain top we viewed the Mediterranean and the Valley of Megiddo. This a most historical battlefield because here many armies of the world have battled through the ages. It was really impressive to watch the place where so many had fought in vain because whether they won or lost it is all now forgotten.

We crossed the valley to Nazareth, where Jesus lived when he was a child. It is in Nazareth where "the child grew and became strong in spirit, filled with wisdom; and the grace of God was upon "Him". Luke 2:40

Arriving at Caesarea Philippi the next morning to view the head-waters of the Jordan River was a delight. We cruised the Sea of Galilee and arrived at Capernaum and visited an ancient synagogue and also Peter's home.

We also visited the Mt of Beatitudes overlooking the sea. What a privilege to be standing on these sacred grounds. It was with much reverence that we all got in our knees and praised our Lord before we opened the Word of God and relived the Sermon on the Mount.

We began the next day with a visit to the Jordan River Baptismal Site. One of our team members had the honor to be baptized at this sight. This was really an occasion to rejoice in remembrance of our Lord's baptism by John the Baptist.

The next day, we crossed the border into Jordan without travail. Our Israeli driver quietly stopped the bus at the border and a Jordanian driver took the wheel. This was done so matter-of-factly that most of us didn't even notice. Next we passed the burial site of Moses at Mt Nebo; saw the crossing where the children of Israel came into the Promised Land toward Jericho.

We had been told that we were going to visit the ruins of Petra, but we were not prepared for the magnificent spectacle we were facing. Petra came alive, out of the rocks, splendorous, powerful and still regal although so many years had passed since it was built.

The terrain was rough and windy, so most of us decided to ride a camel or a donkey. Unfortunately, the camel I was riding decided to quit and promptly stop, folded his legs, and sat sternly without looking at me. Fortunately the guide came to my rescue and helped me un-mount the stubborn beast. I rode a donkey the rest of the way. He was a lot friendlier than his friend, the camel.

From atop the Mount of Olives we saw the fascinating Dome of the Rock and the Garden of Gethsemane. Closing my eyes I pretended to be back in time to listen to my Lord's voice and see Him alive. It was certainly a moment to cherish, to meditate, to glorify and absorb the significance of our journey.

We entered the Old City of Jerusalem through Saint Stephen's Gate. Walking along the Via Dolorosa was more than I could handle. Suddenly I felt terribly sad and confused, I felt a terrible pain and began to quietly sob. I was touched by the fact that I was standing on the same place where He had walked carrying the cross. His tears and His blood had fallen on this same road many years ago and yet, the significance of His death was still alive and permanently imprinted in the lives of every Christian.

By the time we arrived to the climax of our journey, The Garden Tomb, I had regained my composure and was feeling peaceful and calmed. Reflecting on this moment, I later realized, that after the impact of the memories of His death and crucifixion, viewing the empty tomb represented the victory of His resurrection. He is alive, our God is not dead, He is alive!

After this last episode, I was ready to go home. I really wanted to comeback while I was still under the spell, while the experience was still vivid in my memory. Of course this was impossible because my group was not leaving yet, we still had a couple of days left. I also found out later that the Lord had something else planned for me.

I remember visiting the Southern Wall Excavation, praying at the Western Wall, standing on the giant stair that led to the Temple Mount and a few hours shopping at a local market in Jerusalem

It was at this local market, where ancient and modern, secular and religious customs and traditions come together, and the result is a gigantic, vibrant and beautiful place where people come to shop, talk, walk, eat or just look around and enjoy it. However, reality steps in, when you see armed soldiers walking around or just standing, watching the crowds, attentive to every suspicious move, ready to come into action if necessary.

It was here where I had a divine appointment with an Israeli soldier. I was walking around with my best friend and fellow traveler Virginia, looking for souvenirs to bring home. As always happens when we are together, we had brought our Christian tracts and were attentive to every opportunity to witness to people. This time we were explaining the plan of salvation to a couple we had met in one of the shops, when we noticed these two Israeli soldiers looking at us. Our first reaction was to stop what we were doing and hide the tracts, which made us look guilty. However, I noticed that one of the soldiers was smiling at us. Well, I took this as a welcome sign and immediately walked towards him with a big smile and offered him one of the tracts.

To my surprise, he took the tract and started reading it, while his partner stared at both of us. Then he started asking me questions in perfect English. At this moment I stopped thinking rationally, meaning that I ignored the fact that this man represented the Israeli government and was armed, uniformed and on duty. I simply saw a lost soul looking for a savior. I literally forgot where we were and who we were.

All of a sudden it felt like it was just the two of us. After answering his questions and reading a few verses from the Bible I began to pray for His salvation. It was then that he looked at me very seriously and said "that's what I want." The rest was totally supernatural, I held his free hand and asked him to pray with me. He fervently repeated the words I said asking the Lord for forgiveness. He then finished the prayer with his own words, showing repentance for being a sinner and seeking to be pardoned so he could have peace. Again, I forgot he was a uniformed soldier holding a weapon. I put my arms around him and hugged him and he firmly held me and with tears in his eyes, said thank you, thank you.

All the time that this was going on my friend Virginia who had been praying, from afar, rushed over to congratulate our new brother in Christ. We introduced each other and even took pictures and exchanged e-mail addresses and telephone numbers. Meanwhile the other soldier was silently watching everything with a big smile on his face, therefore, I immediately turned to him and asked him if he wanted to pray with me. Still smiling, he said “not now”. And that was it. Before we parted company I asked our new brother to share his new faith with his partner and he said yes. We also gave him two Bibles, one for him and the other one for his partner.

Like I said at the beginning this visit to the Holy Land was a life changing experience for me, now you know why.

BRINGING THE WORD OF GOD TO THE DOMINICAN REPUBLIC

We had been waiting for almost two months and our interest and enthusiasm had grown to the point that we could hardly wait any more for the departure day. This time our Lord was taking us back to a little town in the Dominican Republic where my church was building a school for the local children. This project was a collective effort between the local church and Riverside Baptist, our church in Miami.

Besides providing the material for the construction, every summer our volunteers arrived and donated their labor and their skills. As soon as we arrived our crew was ready to work. They worked very hard finishing the floors, installing windows and doors and taking care of every unfinished detail. Even I got involved in helping the guys laying out the bricks in one of the classrooms. This experience left me totally convinced that with God's help there's is nothing that we cannot do.

A lot had been accomplished already and the building was almost done. This was really a labor of love because our help went beyond their material needs. Most importantly we were building spiritual foundations following our Lord's command to "love the least of these" and "bring the Word of God to every nation".

As any third world community, their material needs were beyond description. We came to help and to provide them with food, medicine, school supplies and clothing, all temporal things that eventually will rot and tear. The real help though, the best and most important thing that we brought to this community was the Love of Jesus. We shared His Word and His love which are eternal gifts destined to grow and forever keep on giving. Like a fountain that will never run dry and a fire that will never die.

Because the local population in this town only spoke Spanish, I had the opportunity to minister in Spanish and also translate for those who did not speak the Spanish language. What a joy it was to deliver the Word of God in Spanish and identify with their culture. Every day I woke up ready to go and eager to receive the blessings of that day.

Ministering to their spiritual needs was by far more rewarding than meeting their physical needs. The joy of bringing one of these souls to the feet of our Lord and seeing the immediate work of the Holy Spirit manifested in their lives was indeed a supernatural experience. Four people gave their lives to Jesus. Among them, a very special soul that the Lord had already filled with His Spirit and was waiting for us. His name was Juan Carlos and his life became an inspiration to his community and a well-taught lesson to the rest of us.

Before we left on the mission, we had prepared a schedule for every day. One of the most innovative ideas that one of our team members had come up with, was a "wordless play" representing the everyday temptations we face and how to deal with them according to His will. We believed that this was a clever way to get the teens involved and teach them the Word of God a different way. We decided to encourage them to perform themselves and challenge them to do it without saying a single word.

We felt confident and anticipated a very successful evening with everyone willing to rehearse by volunteering whatever time it took to learn the different characters and roles to be played.

After many rehearsals we realized we were not making progress on our play. We were tired and restless, but still determined not to give up. The wordless play had become a real challenge because it was difficult to perform. Body language, facial expressions and silent gestures were not enough.

We were committed to reach the audience with this silent message, but something was still missing. I silently prayed "Help us Lord", we want the Torrelindo people to enjoy this play, but most of all, we want them to hear God's Word and be saved! This village spiritual hunger is greater than their material needs. Please help us share Jesus and His love through this beautiful play".

Suddenly, I was brought back from my daydreaming. El Mudo, was walking toward the front, shaking his head and with his hands signaling, No, No, No ! He grabbed a kid, moved him aside and began to act. We were all mesmerized by el Mudo's professional performance. It was simply beautiful, so natural that the play came to life right before our eyes. El Mudo, now in charge, encouraged the others to follow his directions.

Not a word was heard until the play was over. It was then when we realized that a miracle had occurred and we stood up and started clapping. El Mudo got a standing ovation.

I had seen this young man around and had been taken by his beautiful smile and positive attitude. When I asked about him, no one knew his real name. They said everyone called him el Mudo. I sadly realized that he was mostly not noticed except when they were joking around, but was still accepted by his peers because of his kindness and humorous personality

When I asked the Pastor, he confirmed what I already suspected, Jose Pablo, his real name, was borne deaf and mute. Pastor said he felt sorry for him because the boy was unschooled, that he had try to teach him to read and write but it was difficult. He agreed with me that

Jose Pablo had a good mind and a loving heart and that he had accepted Jesus as Lord and Savior. I could tell that the good pastor really care for the boy.

But today it was different; Jose Pablo was not making people laugh. Jose Pablo was making people think and understand God's love for them.

Everything had changed; the other children in the play were asking him questions and paying attention to everything he did.

After the play we prayed and thanked Jesus. The boy leading the prayer prayed for Jose Pablo, this time calling him by name. Afterwards we invited him to dinner to celebrate not only what we had done with his help, but also to pay tribute to the new shining star. Later on in private, I asked the kids to call our friend by his real name, "Jose Pablo". Torrelindo no longer had a "Mudo"

The next morning Jose Pablo told me that his mother was coming to see the play and that he was going to give his best performance. I was so moved by this boy that I hugged him. We were both crying and laughing at the same time.

The night of the play Jose Pablo was the first to arrive with his mother. The lady was radiant, she said that she wanted to meet me and thank me for giving her son the opportunity to do something that made him feel good about himself.

As expected, the play was a total success and everyone was touched by Jose Pablo's performance. This unappreciated and insignificant young man had brought passion and endearment to the occasion and God had shown His love for the little village through one of His most humbled servants.

Before we left, Pastor promised to try to get help for Jose Pablo to learn how to read and write. Because of lack of specialized facilities in these remote villages, people like Jose Pablo don't get the help they need. However, God's love is so perfect that He can reach all of us, no matter who we are or were we live.

VICTORY IN VANCOUVER

We felt victorious, joyful and spiritually energized by what we had just witnessed in Vancouver. The 2010 Winter Olympics had provided us the forum to witness to team members and sport fans from all over the world that had come to enjoy the games. It gave us the unique opportunity to fulfill the Scripture's mission challenge to take the Gospel to the whole world.

Our Answers in Genesis witnessing team of 110 volunteers included more than a dozen Christian teenagers from the U.S. and Canada. This group of young Christians impacted our mission with their love and enthusiasm. They embraced street evangelism with boldness and a tremendous confidence that was certainly inspiring to the rest of us. I am not sure if this figure is record breaking, but on the last day of the Olympic Games one group of three teens and one adult distributed 5,000 booklets.

Our booklet “Gold Rush” presenting the message of salvation, was distributed to more than 92,000 people. Among them were, games participants and international sports fans as well as local residents. This message was presented in seven different languages. It was a delight to see the radiant faces of those who picked up a pamphlet written in their native language. It was an immediate connection and we saw the Spirit of the Lord reaching out to those who had been searching.

Stillwod Camp was the right name for our home for the duration of our mission. This secluded camp not only provided us shelter but also peace and serenity. It was here where each evening our team gathered to share the day’s witnessing opportunities and thanked our God not only for those who were saved, but also those who heard the Word and went home to reflect in solitude to respond later.

Only eternity will reveal the harvest from all the seeds that were planted!

God brought an amazing group to be part of the witness outreach, Christians who were committed to the authority of the Word of God. Our teens with their contagious enthusiasm and total immersion in the Word of God and its healing power were impacting the crowds. They never tired and they shared their love for the Lord with so much joy that it attracted the young and the old, the believers and the unbelievers alike. With a group like this, we were showered with blessings.

We had gathered in the same spot downtown like we did every morning, when I noticed a street vendor selling souvenirs a few feet from us. Since we had just a couple of days left and I had not had a chance to get any Olympic souvenirs for my grandkids back in Florida, I walked over and started looking at the merchandise. When I looked up I saw Choulyn trying to read the logo on my Mounties-red hoodie with a quizzical look on her face. Are you here with one of the teams? She asked. Well, yes......I said taken aback. To which she immediately responded with three more questions: What country? What Sport? And, of course due to my obvious older look. What do you do in your team? Choulyn was smiling and talking real fast while still trying to place a Canadian hockey team bracelet on my arm, which gave me the time to come up with the right answers. I said to her that I had come from the USA with the Jesus Team and that my job was to invite others to join out team.

Choulyn gave me a funny look and laughingly told me to stop joking. Anyway, we both continued laughing and the conversation took off in the right direction. I found out she was a Christian also and that she was happy to know she was already in my team, the "Jesus Team". She said she was from the Philippines and had been a Christian for a long time when she came to Canada from the Philippines and found a good Christian church that she now attended with her family.

I gave her some tracts and asked her if she had something in particular to pray for, to which she said yes, to please pray for one of her customers. This was a man that often came by to shop and talk to her, but since she had found out that he did not believe in God, she had been talking to him about Jesus and praying for him. Of course, I was ready to oblige and we prayed together for her friend to receive the Word of God. When I was ready to go back to my group she insisted on giving me the bracelet as a gift and would not take no for an answer.

The next day I was with my team at a different venue. We were talking to some young Christians from Russia who were also ministering at the games, when one of my partners from another team came rushing to tell me that the vendor lady was looking for me. He said that Choulyn wanted me to come by before going home that day. My friend added that Choulyn was afraid that I would leave Vancouver before we could meet again. He added that she was so determined to see me that she wanted to know the camp address just in case.

For some reason I was not surprised because she had really impressed me with her genuine concern for her friend's soul and I was hoping to see her again and pray with her before we left Canada. Also when we went back to camp the day before, I shared her story with my team and we had all prayed for both of them.

I looked forward to the meeting with my new friend all day long and that evening as I was walking towards her, she saw me and ran to meet me. She was very happy and immediately began to tell me that her friend had been there earlier and that she had ask him to please comeback later that evening because she wanted him to meet me. She asked me to please wait that she was sure he would return as he had promised to do.

We had been talking for just a few minutes when her friend arrived. From then on everything began to happen as if it had been previously rehearsed. The gentleman was well dressed and very polite. He said his name was Ernest and that he was English but had lived in Canada since he was a child. He added that he had comeback only because Choulyn was so convincing that got him curious enough to return and meet me, but that he had a good idea that it had something to do with "religion." We both nervously laughed and introduced ourselves, while Choulyn was joking around trying to make everyone feel comfortable.

Anyway, here is when the unexpected happened. The gentleman started asking questions and really paying attention to my answers. Suddenly though he stop and thanked me, adding that he had heard it all before. I was perplexed. I guess I had anticipated a totally different outcome, but he had not given me the chance to talk about Jesus and His love, the real message I wanted to deliver. I really wondered why Ernest had return when he knew his mind was already made up. Still I wouldn't give up and offered him a Bible and some tracts, but he politely refused to take them.

Choulyn, equally surprised, stood next to me obviously very disappointed and uncharacteristically quiet. Finally, Ernest said he had to go and we politely shook hands. He said goodbye to both of us and began to walk away. He had not walked but a few steps, when he turned around and asked me to give him the Bible I had just offered him. By now I had regained my composure and eagerly handed him the Bible with a big smile and softly said to him "God Bless you Ernest". He smiled back and said "thank you maam". He left and we stood there both smiling and waiving goodbye. The fact that Ernest had asked to take the Bible with him was very significant and it restored our hopes. Choulyn and I held each other in a tight embrace and promised to keep in touch and keep praying for each other and also for Ernest.

It is time for reflection now, but my excitement has not subsided. I cannot forget the multitude of people, walking around aimlessly seeking, searching, looking for something or someone to satisfy their inner craving for fulfillment, completeness or closure. In other words, "the human desire to fill the God-shaped vacuum in each of our hearts". This is why I still want to shout..............JESUS CHRIST IS WHAT YOU ARE LOOKING FOR!

Sadly, they don't know what they are looking for. Thus the search continues until they hear the Word and then make the choice to repent and live or be eternally condemned to Hell! Here is where we come in. We, the followers of Christ are the ones who were chosen to bring the Message of Salvation to those who are waiting to hear the Word of God.

Dear Brothers and Sisters in Christ, I appeal to you to fulfill the Great Commission! Each one of us has been appointed by God to bring these blessed souls the Good News of Jesus Christ and His love. The Scriptures are being fulfilled, the time is now, the harvest is ready and we need many workers. Think and be encouraged by the thought that we have to meet "divine appointments" already predestined by our Lord.

He is speaking to each one of us when He says "follow me". This is the time to obey, to leave behind material treasures and everything that keeps us attached to the world and follow HIM. The time is NOW the harvest is READY, the souls are WAITING, Let's GO!

After this clear exhortation I am hoping that you, the reader by the grace of God receives and accepts His command to the extent that it would prompt you to make a personal commitment. Remember, the fields are ripe for harvest. The sower and the reaper rejoice together because sometimes the Lord allows us to reap that for which we have not labored.

GUATEMALA READY FOR JESUS

"And the grace of our Lord was exceedingly abundant." I Timothy 1:14 Like water from a fountain, His saving grace was flowing from the mountains to the valleys, reaching the towns and the cities and all over the land. And the people were eagerly drinking the Living Water because they knew that they would never thirst again.

All ten of us soon realized that this mission was special. From the very beginning we all felt the presence of the Holy Spirit among us. Led by Brother John, we began each day with prayer and thanksgiving, worshiping our Lord and asking for His guidance and protection. Every one of us was in perfect peace and communion with our Lord. We knew that we were here because it was God's plan for us, including our two teens, Josh and Javi who had so eagerly volunteered to come.

Never did we fear the many dangers that we were told we might encounter. The droves of mosquitoes never appeared. A few solitary "zancudos" (mosquitoes in Spanish) came by but never bothered us. It never rained and although the temperature remained in the nineties day and night, we soon learned to live with it and without air conditioning.

The only time we really felt challenged was when we drove on an old and dangerous road alongside the mountains, from a city called Puerto Barrios to the little towns of San Miguelito and Las Escobas. The one-lane, mostly unpaved road, was even more dangerous because of the many old trucks and trailers driving through at high speed, ignoring traffic signals, if any, and unconcerned about the narrow passage we were traveling on. The only consolation for my traveling sister in Christ, Betty, and I, was that we had eight strong and healthy men in our team, ready to pick up the van and carry it if necessary.

We braced ourselves when we faced imminent danger, but otherwise entertained ourselves pretty well by eating, telling jokes, playing games and singing hymns. We prayed fervently and invoked the name of Jesus to protect us. We also tried not to look out the window to avoid seeing the scary abyss at the edge of the mountain road. I can honestly say that regardless of the danger we might have encountered, we all had peace, the peace that surpasses all understanding.

The beauty of the naturally primitive environment was only surpassed by the beauty of the people, especially the children. Their smiling faces reflected the genuine joy they felt when we arrived at the schools. They were eagerly expecting us and were ready to accept anything we brought for them.

We had been instructed by Dr. Ken to make a presentation emphasizing the need to prevent contagious diseases and to discuss the different ways these diseases spread, especially those transmitted by mosquitoes, like dengue fever and malaria. Afterwards, younger team members illustrated how this happens with the help of a puppet show. The puppets were a hit! The kids eagerly participated in the discussion and ultimately, I believe learning did occurred.

After singing some Spanish "coritos" (short Christian songs) we had learned and accompanied by one of our young team members playing his ukulele we were ready to introduce the most important member of our team, our Lord Jesus Christ. Although very few of the children had knowledge of Jesus and His salvation, they quietly listened and paid attention to every word we said. We had brought with us the "color beaded bracelets" illustrating the Plan of Salvation, and shared it with the children. Everyone in the room was mesmerized by the story of Jesus and His love, including the teachers. The class willingly participated by asking and answering questions.

We visited a total of six schools in three days and talked to approximately a thousand children. Each classroom held about 50 children. They sat closely next to each other and although the windows were open the temperature in the room remained almost unbearable, no one complained. The children were well behaved and paid attention to everything we said. Their desire to learn was evident. After the classes were over Javi and Josh were ready to accept their new friends' invitation to play soccer or "futbol" as it is locally called. It was wonderful to see them play and have a good time together.

When we returned to Puerto Barrios we went to the Baptist Church that had invited us. Led by their Pastor and some church members, we visited many homes and invited the families to attend a Church service the following day.

Unknown to us, we had visited and invited to the service, two ladies who lived across the street from the church who had been a little difficult in the past. However, when we went to their home they were pleasant and even invited us to come in and attentively listened to us when we prayed for them. They also accepted our invitation to come and join us at our church for the next day evening service..

When we learned that they had voiced several complaints in the past about the services being too loud and too long and cars parked on their property etc, we were really surprised, but at the same time happy that we had invited them. That same night during our evening prayers, we specifically prayed for these ladies and asked the Holy Spirit to minister to them.

This is why we were not really surprised when the next evening they came to pray and worship the Lord with us. The pastor was very happy to see them, and immediately welcomed his old neighbors and new friends with much enthusiasm. I can say with certainty that the feeling was mutual, both ladies were smiling and talking and evidently very glad to be in the little church. One again, we see how people are changed when they listen to the Word of God, even when they are not actively seeking Him. Blessed be the Lord !

After the service we had the puppet show for the children and also presented a drama that depicted how man is led to sin by the many temptations around him and the redeeming power of Jesus Christ, the only way we can obtain salvation. This drama was very well accepted by the audience. We observed some people crying. Again, we were pleased with the outcome. People stayed after the service to ask questions and to ask us to pray for them.

When we finally returned to the capital, Guatemala City, we were pleased with the results. We figured we had given away at least 500 Bibles, many tracts in Spanish and Josh's ukulele. We had also shared the word of God with hundreds of souls. Although we realized that the real success of this mission was probably not going to be revealed until we meet again in Heaven, we felt spiritually satisfied. We had been obedient to the Lord when He entrusted us to fulfill the Great Commission, and in the process we were transformed.

SECTION TWO

++++++

DEDICATED

TO THE ONE I LOVE

Do You Hear The Cry Of the Lost?

Walking up and down the earth
unsaved souls in great despair
crying out loud, but their voices unheard
some are giving up, but some still search

Always reminded of their own mistakes
they wander in vain, but cannot escape,
the weight of their sins driving them insane,
while hopelessly trying to save themselves

Do you hear their cry, the lone preacher says
if you really listen, you will hear their pain
voices in the wilderness, calling in distress
wishing to be rescued, failing to be heard

Once you hear their cry, you cannot forget
the Cry of the Lost, invading your thoughts
incessantly pleading to find what they lost
oblivious to the one they nailed to the Cross

Once you hear their cry, you come to realize
that when you know Jesus you cannot deny
that it is our mission, commanded by God
to leave our comfort and rescue these souls

Do you Hear the Cry of the Lost?
This time we all must go.
The lost souls are waiting,
to be rescued and be told,
that Jesus is the answer
that they're looking for

Maria Booth

Gladys "Maria" Sotomayor Booth is a USA veteran who retired from the U.S.Department of Defense after 30-years of civil service. Since her retirement, she has dedicated her life to travel to different countries around the world and share with them the Gospel of Jesus Christ and His love.

CPSIA information can be obtained at www.ICGtesting.com
Printed in the USA
LVOW040356291211

261457LV00001B/5/P